EMMANUEL JOSEPH

The Disruption DNA, How Billionaires Code Industries for Revolution and Redraw the Globe

Copyright © 2025 by Emmanuel Joseph

All rights reserved. No part of this publication may be reproduced, stored or transmitted in any form or by any means, electronic, mechanical, photocopying, recording, scanning, or otherwise without written permission from the publisher. It is illegal to copy this book, post it to a website, or distribute it by any other means without permission.

First edition

This book was professionally typeset on Reedsy. Find out more at reedsy.com

Contents

1	Chapter 1: The Disruption Phenomenon	1
2	Chapter 2: Visionary Thinking	3
3	Chapter 3: Technological Prowess	5
4	Chapter 4: Strategic Risk-Taking	7
5	Chapter 5: The Power of Networks	9
6	Chapter 6: Market Sensing	11
7	Chapter 7: Strategic Agility	13
8	Chapter 8: Financial Acumen	15
9	Chapter 9: Customer-Centric Innovation	17
10	Chapter 10: Ethical Leadership	19
11	Chapter 11: The Role of Resilience	21
12	Chapter 12: The Impact of Disruption on Society	23
13	Chapter 13: The Global Reach of Disruption	25
14	Chapter 14: The Role of Policy and Regulation	27
15	Chapter 15: Building a Legacy	29
16	Chapter 16: Lessons from Disruptive Billionaires	31
17	Chapter 17: The Future of Disruption	33

1

Chapter 1: The Disruption Phenomenon

In the fast-paced, ever-evolving landscape of the modern economy, disruption has become a buzzword synonymous with innovation and transformation. This phenomenon is not merely a fleeting trend but a fundamental shift in how industries operate and grow. At its core, disruption is driven by individuals and companies that challenge the status quo, offering radical alternatives that redefine market expectations. The impact of such disruption is both profound and far-reaching, often leading to the obsolescence of established players and the emergence of new leaders.

Billionaires who master the art of disruption possess a unique blend of visionary thinking and practical execution. These individuals are not content with incremental improvements; instead, they seek to revolutionize entire industries by leveraging cutting-edge technologies and novel business models. Their ability to foresee market shifts and capitalize on emerging opportunities sets them apart from the rest. By pushing the boundaries of what is possible, these disruptors create a ripple effect that reshapes the global economic landscape.

The DNA of disruption is characterized by a relentless pursuit of innovation, a willingness to take risks, and an unwavering commitment to challenging conventional wisdom. This mindset is not limited to a specific industry but transcends sectors, from technology and finance to healthcare and transportation. The most successful disruptors understand that true innovation requires a departure from traditional methods and a willingness to embrace the unknown. They are unafraid to fail, viewing setbacks as opportunities for growth and learning.

As we delve deeper into the world of disruptive billionaires, it becomes clear that their impact extends beyond mere financial success. These individuals are catalysts for change, driving societal progress and shaping the future in ways that benefit humanity as a whole. By decoding the principles and strategies that underpin their success, we can gain valuable insights into the dynamics of disruption and learn how to harness its power to drive positive transformation.

2

Chapter 2: Visionary Thinking

At the heart of every successful disruptor lies a powerful vision that serves as the driving force behind their endeavors. This vision is not just a lofty goal but a clear and compelling picture of what the future could be. Visionary thinking involves the ability to see beyond the present and anticipate trends, challenges, and opportunities that others might overlook. It is this foresight that enables disruptors to stay ahead of the curve and position themselves as pioneers in their respective fields.

Billionaires who excel in disruptive innovation possess an uncanny ability to identify gaps in the market and envision solutions that address unmet needs. Their vision is often rooted in a deep understanding of the industry landscape, coupled with a keen awareness of technological advancements and societal shifts. This holistic perspective allows them to connect the dots in ways that others cannot, creating a roadmap for revolutionary change.

A key aspect of visionary thinking is the capacity to inspire and mobilize others around a shared purpose. Disruptors are adept at articulating their vision in a way that resonates with stakeholders, from employees and investors to customers and partners. This ability to rally support and build a strong network of collaborators is crucial for turning visionary ideas into reality. By fostering a culture of innovation and encouraging diverse perspectives, disruptors create an environment where groundbreaking ideas can flourish.

While visionary thinking is often associated with bold and ambitious goals, it is also grounded in practicality. Successful disruptors understand the importance of execution and are skilled at translating their vision into actionable strategies. They are adept at balancing long-term aspirations with short-term priorities, ensuring that their vision is not just a dream but a tangible path to success. This combination of visionary thinking and pragmatic execution is what sets disruptive billionaires apart from the rest.

3

Chapter 3: Technological Prowess

In the age of rapid technological advancement, the ability to harness and leverage cutting-edge technologies is a defining characteristic of disruptive billionaires. These individuals are not just consumers of technology but pioneers who push the boundaries of what is possible. Their deep understanding of emerging technologies, from artificial intelligence and blockchain to biotechnology and renewable energy, enables them to create innovative solutions that transform industries and improve lives.

Disruptors recognize that technology is a powerful tool for driving change and are relentless in their pursuit of technological excellence. They invest heavily in research and development, constantly exploring new ways to integrate technology into their business models. This commitment to innovation allows them to stay ahead of the competition and maintain a competitive edge in the market. By embracing technological advancements, disruptors can create products and services that are more efficient, effective, and accessible.

One of the key strengths of disruptive billionaires is their ability to anticipate the impact of technological trends and adapt accordingly. They are not content with merely keeping up with the latest developments; instead, they seek to shape the future by setting new standards and driving the adoption of groundbreaking technologies. This forward-thinking approach requires a deep understanding of the potential applications and implications of technology, as well as the ability to navigate the complex and ever-changing landscape of the tech industry.

The technological prowess of disruptors is complemented by their willingness to take calculated risks. They understand that innovation often involves venturing into uncharted territory and are unafraid to experiment with new ideas and approaches. This risk-taking mindset is essential for pushing the boundaries of what is possible and achieving breakthroughs that redefine industries. By fostering a culture of experimentation and learning, disruptive billionaires create an environment where technological innovation can thrive.

4

Chapter 4: Strategic Risk-Taking

At the core of disruptive innovation lies a willingness to take risks and embrace uncertainty. Billionaires who excel in disruption understand that playing it safe is not an option when it comes to driving revolutionary change. Instead, they adopt a strategic approach to risk-taking, carefully weighing the potential rewards against the inherent uncertainties. This calculated approach allows them to make bold moves that propel their businesses forward and set them apart from the competition.

Strategic risk-taking involves a combination of intuition, analysis, and decisiveness. Disruptors possess a keen ability to identify opportunities that others might consider too risky or unfeasible. They rely on their intuition to sense emerging trends and shifts in the market, while also conducting thorough analysis to assess the potential impact and feasibility of their ideas. This blend of instinct and data-driven decision-making enables them to navigate the uncertainties of disruptive innovation with confidence.

One of the hallmarks of successful disruptors is their resilience in the face of failure. They understand that not every risk will yield positive results and are prepared to learn from their mistakes. Rather than being discouraged by setbacks, they view them as valuable learning experiences that provide insights for future endeavors. This ability to bounce back from failure and iterate on their ideas is a critical component of their success. By maintaining a growth mindset and continuously refining their strategies, disruptors are able to turn challenges into opportunities.

Another key aspect of strategic risk-taking is the ability to build and leverage a strong support network. Disruptors recognize the importance of surrounding themselves with individuals who share their vision and can provide valuable perspectives and expertise. This network includes mentors, advisors, investors, and partners who can offer guidance and support throughout the disruptive journey. By fostering collaborative relationships and creating a culture of trust and mutual respect, disruptors are able to mitigate risks and maximize their chances of success.

5

Chapter 5: The Power of Networks

In the interconnected world of today, the power of networks cannot be overstated. Disruptive billionaires understand that building and leveraging strong networks is essential for driving innovation and achieving sustained success. These networks encompass a diverse range of stakeholders, from employees and customers to investors, partners, and industry influencers. By cultivating meaningful relationships and creating synergies, disruptors are able to amplify their impact and accelerate their growth.

One of the key strengths of disruptive billionaires is their ability to attract and retain top talent. They understand that innovation is a team effort and that having the right people on board is crucial for turning visionary ideas into reality. Disruptors create a culture of collaboration and empowerment, where individuals are encouraged to contribute their unique skills and perspectives. By fostering a sense of ownership and purpose, they inspire their teams to push the boundaries of what is possible.

In addition to building strong internal networks, disruptors also recognize the importance of external relationships. They actively seek out partnerships and alliances that can help them achieve their goals and drive industry-wide change. These collaborations often involve working with other innovative companies, research institutions, and industry organizations. By leveraging the strengths and expertise of their partners, disruptors are able to achieve breakthroughs that would not be possible on their own.

The power of networks extends beyond the immediate business environment. Disruptive billionaires understand that their success is closely tied to the broader ecosystem in which they operate. They engage with industry influencers, policymakers, and thought leaders to shape the future direction of their industries. By actively participating in industry forums, conferences, and other platforms, disruptors are able to share their insights, influence policy decisions, and drive positive change. This proactive approach to networking allows them to stay ahead of the curve and maintain a competitive edge.

6

Chapter 6: Market Sensing

The ability to sense and respond to market changes is a critical skill for disruptive billionaires. Market sensing involves a deep understanding of customer needs, preferences, and behaviors, as well as an awareness of emerging trends and competitive dynamics. Disruptors are adept at gathering and analyzing market intelligence to identify opportunities and threats, enabling them to make informed decisions and stay ahead of the competition.

Disruptive billionaires prioritize customer-centricity in their market sensing efforts. They recognize that understanding the customer is key to delivering innovative solutions that meet their needs and exceed their expectations. Disruptors invest in market research, customer feedback, and data analytics to gain insights into customer pain points and preferences. This customer-centric approach allows them to tailor their offerings and create products and services that resonate with their target audience.

In addition to understanding customer needs, disruptors also keep a close eye on industry trends and competitive developments. They leverage various sources of information, including market reports, industry publications, and social media, to stay informed about the latest happenings in their field. This proactive approach to market sensing allows them to identify emerging opportunities and pivot their strategies as needed to maintain a competitive edge.

Disruptive billionaires are skilled at interpreting market signals and turning insights into action. They have a knack for identifying patterns and trends that others might overlook, enabling them to make strategic decisions with confidence. This ability to read the market landscape and anticipate changes is a critical component of their success. By staying agile and responsive, disruptors can quickly adapt to shifting market dynamics and seize new opportunities.

Another important aspect of market sensing is the ability to foster a culture of continuous learning and innovation within the organization. Disruptors encourage their teams to stay curious and informed about industry developments, creating an environment where new ideas are welcomed and explored. This commitment to ongoing learning ensures that the organization remains at the forefront of innovation and is well-positioned to capitalize on emerging trends.

Ultimately, market sensing is about staying one step ahead of the competition by constantly scanning the horizon for new opportunities and potential threats. Disruptive billionaires understand that the ability to adapt and evolve is key to long-term success. By maintaining a keen awareness of the market landscape and staying attuned to customer needs, they can continue to drive innovation and create value for their stakeholders.

7

Chapter 7: Strategic Agility

In a rapidly changing business environment, strategic agility is a crucial trait for disruptive billionaires. This ability to quickly adapt and pivot in response to new information and changing circumstances sets them apart from their more rigid counterparts. Strategic agility involves a combination of flexibility, foresight, and decisive action, enabling disruptors to navigate uncertainty and capitalize on emerging opportunities.

Disruptors understand that long-term success requires the ability to anticipate and respond to shifts in the market. They are constantly scanning the horizon for potential changes and assessing their impact on the business. This proactive approach allows them to stay ahead of the curve and make informed decisions that drive growth and innovation. By maintaining a flexible mindset and being open to change, disruptors can navigate the complexities of the modern business landscape with confidence.

One of the key elements of strategic agility is the ability to make quick and informed decisions. Disruptive billionaires are skilled at analyzing data and assessing risks, enabling them to make bold moves with confidence. They understand that hesitation can lead to missed opportunities, so they prioritize decisive action while remaining mindful of potential risks. This balance between speed and caution is essential for driving innovation and staying ahead of the competition.

Strategic agility also involves the ability to pivot when necessary. Disruptors are not wedded to a single strategy or business model; instead, they are willing to change course if the situation demands it. This willingness to adapt and evolve is a key factor in their success. By staying nimble and responsive, disruptors can seize new opportunities and overcome challenges as they arise. This ability to pivot and adapt ensures that they remain at the forefront of their industries and continue to drive revolutionary change.

8

Chapter 8: Financial Acumen

A keen understanding of finance is another defining trait of disruptive billionaires. Their ability to manage resources, attract investment, and drive profitability is a critical component of their success. Financial acumen involves a deep understanding of financial principles, as well as the ability to make strategic decisions that maximize value for stakeholders. Disruptors leverage their financial expertise to fuel growth, drive innovation, and achieve long-term success.

Disruptive billionaires are skilled at identifying and capitalizing on investment opportunities. They understand the importance of securing funding to support their innovative endeavors and are adept at attracting investment from a variety of sources. Whether through venture capital, private equity, or strategic partnerships, disruptors have a knack for securing the resources needed to bring their visionary ideas to life. This ability to attract and manage investment is a key factor in their ability to drive revolutionary change.

In addition to attracting investment, disruptors are also skilled at managing financial resources. They understand the importance of budgeting, forecasting, and financial planning to ensure the long-term sustainability of their businesses. Disruptors prioritize financial discipline, making strategic decisions that balance short-term needs with long-term goals. This focus on financial management allows them to navigate the complexities of the business landscape and maintain a competitive edge.

Financial acumen also involves the ability to drive profitability and create value for stakeholders. Disruptors understand that financial success is not just about revenue growth but also about delivering value to customers, employees, and investors. They are adept at identifying opportunities for cost savings, optimizing operations, and driving efficiencies that enhance profitability. By maintaining a focus on financial performance, disruptors can achieve sustained success and continue to drive innovation in their industries.

9

Chapter 9: Customer-Centric Innovation

Customer-centric innovation is at the heart of disruptive billionaires' success. These individuals understand that delivering value to customers is the key to driving growth and achieving long-term success. Customer-centric innovation involves a deep understanding of customer needs and preferences, as well as the ability to develop products and services that address those needs in new and innovative ways.

Disruptors prioritize customer feedback and actively seek out insights that can inform their innovation efforts. They invest in market research, customer surveys, and data analytics to gain a comprehensive understanding of their target audience. This customer-centric approach allows them to develop solutions that resonate with customers and create lasting value. By staying attuned to customer needs, disruptors can drive innovation and maintain a competitive edge.

In addition to understanding customer needs, disruptors also focus on delivering exceptional customer experiences. They recognize that customer satisfaction is a key driver of loyalty and advocacy. Disruptors invest in customer service, user experience design, and other initiatives that enhance the overall customer journey. By prioritizing the customer experience, disruptors can build strong relationships with their customers and create a loyal customer base.

Customer-centric innovation also involves the ability to anticipate and respond to changing customer needs. Disruptors are skilled at identifying emerging trends and adapting their offerings to meet evolving customer demands. This ability to stay ahead of the curve and deliver innovative solutions that address new and emerging needs is a key factor in their success. By maintaining a customer-centric focus, disruptors can continue to drive growth and create value in their industries.

10

Chapter 10: Ethical Leadership

Ethical leadership is a cornerstone of disruptive billionaires' success. These individuals understand that driving innovation and achieving long-term success requires a commitment to ethical principles and responsible business practices. Ethical leadership involves a focus on integrity, transparency, and accountability, as well as a commitment to making a positive impact on society.

Disruptors prioritize ethical decision-making and hold themselves to high standards of conduct. They understand that their actions have far-reaching implications and strive to make decisions that are in the best interests of their stakeholders. This commitment to ethical leadership builds trust and credibility with customers, employees, investors, and other stakeholders. By prioritizing ethical behavior, disruptors can create a strong foundation for sustained success.

In addition to ethical decision-making, disruptors also focus on corporate social responsibility (CSR). They recognize that businesses have a responsibility to contribute to the well-being of society and the environment. Disruptors invest in initiatives that promote sustainability, social equity, and community engagement. By prioritizing CSR, disruptors can create positive social impact and build a strong reputation as responsible corporate citizens.

Ethical leadership also involves a commitment to transparency and accountability. Disruptors prioritize open and honest communication with their stakeholders, providing regular updates on their performance and progress. They are willing to acknowledge and address challenges and setbacks, demonstrating a commitment to continuous improvement. This focus on transparency and accountability builds trust and fosters a culture of integrity within the organization.

Ultimately, ethical leadership is about creating value for all stakeholders while driving innovation and achieving long-term success. Disruptors understand that ethical behavior is not just a moral imperative but also a key driver of business success. By prioritizing ethical leadership, they can create a positive and sustainable impact on society and the economy.

11

Chapter 11: The Role of Resilience

Resilience is a critical trait for disruptive billionaires, enabling them to navigate the challenges and uncertainties of the business landscape. Resilience involves the ability to recover from setbacks, adapt to changing circumstances, and maintain a positive outlook in the face of adversity. Disruptors understand that failure is an inevitable part of the innovation journey and are prepared to learn from their experiences and keep moving forward.

Disruptive billionaires possess a growth mindset, viewing challenges and failures as opportunities for learning and improvement. They understand that resilience is not just about bouncing back from setbacks but also about continuously adapting and evolving in response to new information and changing conditions. This ability to stay agile and responsive is a key factor in their success. By maintaining a growth mindset and embracing change, disruptors can navigate the complexities of the business landscape with confidence.

Another important aspect of resilience is the ability to stay focused and motivated in the face of adversity. Disruptors are driven by a strong sense of purpose and a deep commitment to their vision. This inner drive enables them to persevere through challenges and setbacks, maintaining their focus on their long-term goals. By staying motivated and focused, disruptors can overcome obstacles and continue to drive innovation and growth.

Resilience also involves the ability to build and maintain a strong support network. Disruptors understand that resilience is not just an individual trait but also a collective effort. They surround themselves with individuals who share their vision and can provide valuable support and encouragement. This network includes mentors, advisors, investors, and partners who can offer guidance and support during challenging times. By fostering strong relationships and creating a culture of support, disruptors can build resilience within their organizations and achieve sustained success.

Ultimately, resilience is about maintaining a positive outlook and a commitment to continuous improvement. Disruptors understand that the path to resilience is about maintaining a positive outlook and a commitment to continuous improvement. Disruptors understand that the path to innovation and success is rarely straightforward and that resilience is essential for navigating the ups and downs of the journey. By staying resilient and focused on their long-term vision, disruptors can overcome challenges and continue to drive revolutionary change.

12

Chapter 12: The Impact of Disruption on Society

Disruptive innovation does not exist in a vacuum; it has far-reaching implications for society as a whole. Billionaires who drive disruptive change understand that their actions can have a profound impact on various aspects of society, from the economy and job market to education and healthcare. By leveraging their influence and resources, disruptors can drive positive social change and contribute to the betterment of society.

One of the key ways in which disruption impacts society is through the creation of new industries and job opportunities. Disruptors often introduce new technologies and business models that generate demand for new skills and expertise. This can lead to the creation of new job opportunities and the transformation of existing industries. However, it is important for disruptors to also consider the potential impact on displaced workers and invest in initiatives that support workforce development and retraining.

Disruptive innovation can also drive improvements in access to essential services such as healthcare and education. By leveraging technology and innovative approaches, disruptors can create solutions that are more affordable, efficient, and accessible. For example, telemedicine and online education platforms have the potential to reach underserved populations and improve access to quality healthcare and education. By prioritizing social impact, disruptors can create solutions that address pressing societal challenges and improve the quality of life for people around the world.

Another important aspect of the societal impact of disruption is the potential for driving sustainability and environmental stewardship. Disruptors who prioritize sustainability can create innovative solutions that reduce environmental impact and promote a more sustainable future. For example, advancements in renewable energy, sustainable agriculture, and circular economy models have the potential to address pressing environmental challenges and drive positive change. By leveraging their influence and resources, disruptors can lead the way in creating a more sustainable and equitable world.

13

Chapter 13: The Global Reach of Disruption

In today's interconnected world, the impact of disruptive innovation extends beyond national borders. Disruptive billionaires understand that their actions can have a global reach, influencing markets and societies around the world. By leveraging their global networks and resources, disruptors can drive innovation and create value on a global scale.

One of the key drivers of the global reach of disruption is the rapid advancement of technology. Innovations in communication, transportation, and information technology have made it easier than ever for disruptors to reach new markets and connect with customers and partners around the world. This global connectivity allows disruptors to scale their innovations and create impact on a larger scale. By leveraging technology and global networks, disruptors can drive revolutionary change that transcends geographic boundaries.

The global reach of disruption also involves the ability to navigate diverse cultural, regulatory, and economic landscapes. Disruptive billionaires are skilled at understanding and adapting to the unique challenges and opportunities presented by different regions and markets. They invest in building strong relationships with local stakeholders and understanding the specific needs and preferences of their target audiences. This ability to navigate global complexities is a key factor in their success. By fostering cross-cultural understanding and collaboration, disruptors can create solutions that are relevant and impactful in diverse contexts.

Another important aspect of the global reach of disruption is the potential for driving inclusive growth and development. Disruptors who prioritize inclusivity can create solutions that address the needs of underserved populations and promote economic and social development. For example, innovations in financial technology, healthcare, and education have the potential to improve access to essential services and create new opportunities for people around the world. By leveraging their global reach, disruptors can create positive impact and contribute to a more equitable and inclusive world.

14

Chapter 14: The Role of Policy and Regulation

The role of policy and regulation in shaping the landscape of disruptive innovation cannot be underestimated. Disruptive billionaires understand that navigating the regulatory environment is essential for driving innovation and achieving sustained success. By engaging with policymakers and regulators, disruptors can influence the development of policies that support innovation and create a conducive environment for disruptive change.

One of the key challenges faced by disruptors is the need to balance innovation with regulatory compliance. Disruptive innovations often challenge existing regulatory frameworks and create new questions and uncertainties. Disruptors who are proactive in engaging with regulators and policymakers can help shape the development of policies that address these challenges and support the growth of new industries. By fostering a collaborative relationship with regulators, disruptors can create an environment that encourages innovation while ensuring public safety and trust.

Disruptive billionaires also recognize the importance of advocating for policies that promote competition and prevent monopolistic practices. By supporting policies that encourage fair competition, disruptors can create a level playing field that fosters innovation and benefits consumers. This commitment to promoting competition is essential for driving industry-wide change and creating a dynamic and innovative market environment.

In addition to engaging with policymakers, disruptors also play a key role in advocating for ethical and responsible business practices. They understand that policies and regulations can help ensure that innovation is conducted in a way that prioritizes social and environmental responsibility. By advocating for policies that promote sustainability, social equity, and ethical behavior, disruptors can create a positive impact on society and contribute to the development of a more responsible and inclusive business environment.

Ultimately, the role of policy and regulation in shaping the landscape of disruptive innovation is a collaborative effort. Disruptive billionaires who engage with policymakers and regulators can help create a regulatory environment that supports innovation while ensuring public trust and safety. By fostering a collaborative relationship with regulators and advocating for responsible business practices, disruptors can drive positive change and create a more dynamic and innovative market environment.

15

Chapter 15: Building a Legacy

For disruptive billionaires, building a lasting legacy is about more than just financial success; it is about creating a positive and enduring impact on the world. This involves a commitment to innovation, ethical leadership, and social responsibility. By prioritizing these principles, disruptors can create a legacy that extends beyond their individual achievements and contributes to the betterment of society.

One of the key elements of building a legacy is the ability to drive positive social change. Disruptive billionaires understand that their success provides them with a platform to make a difference in the world. They leverage their influence and resources to address pressing societal challenges and create solutions that improve the quality of life for people around the world. This commitment to social impact is a defining characteristic of their legacy.

In addition to driving social change, disruptors also focus on fostering a culture of innovation and continuous improvement. They understand that their legacy is not just about their individual achievements but also about the impact they have on their organizations and industries. Disruptors invest in building strong teams and creating an environment where innovation can thrive. By fostering a culture of curiosity, collaboration, and learning, disruptors ensure that their organizations continue to drive innovation and create value long after they are gone.

Another important aspect of building a legacy is the commitment to ethical leadership and responsible business practices. Disruptive billionaires understand that their actions have far-reaching implications and strive to make decisions that are in the best interests of their stakeholders. By prioritizing ethical behavior and responsible business practices, disruptors can build trust and credibility with their stakeholders and create a strong foundation for sustained success.

Ultimately, building a legacy is about creating a positive and lasting impact on the world. Disruptive billionaires who prioritize innovation, ethical leadership, and social responsibility can create a legacy that extends beyond their individual achievements and contributes to the betterment of society. By staying true to their values and driving positive change, disruptors can leave a lasting mark on the world and inspire future generations to follow in their footsteps.

16

Chapter 16: Lessons from Disruptive Billionaires

The journey of disruptive billionaires offers valuable lessons for aspiring innovators and entrepreneurs. These lessons are rooted in the principles and strategies that have driven their success and can provide valuable insights for those looking to drive revolutionary change in their own industries.

One of the key lessons from disruptive billionaires is the importance of visionary thinking. Disruptors possess a clear and compelling vision that guides their actions and inspires others. Aspiring innovators can learn from this by developing a strong vision for their own endeavors and staying focused on their long-term goals. By maintaining a clear sense of purpose and direction, they can navigate the challenges and uncertainties of the innovation journey with confidence.

Another important lesson is the value of strategic risk-taking. Disruptive billionaires understand that innovation often involves venturing into uncharted territory and are willing to take calculated risks. Aspiring innovators can learn from this by being open to new ideas and approaches, and by viewing setbacks as opportunities for learning and growth. By staying resilient and embracing risk, they can drive innovation and achieve success.

The role of customer-centric innovation is another valuable lesson from disruptive billionaires. Disruptors prioritize understanding and addressing customer needs, creating solutions that deliver value and exceed expectations. Aspiring innovators can learn from this by staying attuned to customer feedback and investing in market research and data analytics. By maintaining a customer-centric focus, they can develop products and services that resonate with their target audience and drive growth.

Finally, the importance of ethical leadership and social responsibility is a key lesson from disruptive billionaires. Disruptors understand that driving innovation and achieving long-term success requires a commitment to ethical principles and responsible business practices. Aspiring innovators can learn from this by prioritizing integrity, transparency, and accountability in their own endeavors. By making decisions that are in the best interests of their stakeholders and contributing to the betterment of society, they can build a strong foundation for sustained success.

17

Chapter 17: The Future of Disruption

As we look to the future, the role of disruptive innovation in shaping the global economy and society will only continue to grow. Disruptive billionaires will continue to drive revolutionary change, leveraging their visionary thinking, technological prowess, and ethical leadership to create a positive impact on society. The future of disruption will be shaped by a confluence of factors, including advancements in technology, shifting consumer behaviors, and evolving societal needs. As new challenges and opportunities emerge, disruptive billionaires will continue to play a pivotal role in driving innovation and shaping the global economy.

One of the key trends that will shape the future of disruption is the rise of artificial intelligence and machine learning. These technologies have the potential to revolutionize a wide range of industries, from healthcare and finance to transportation and manufacturing. Disruptors who can harness the power of AI and machine learning will be well-positioned to create innovative solutions that address complex challenges and unlock new opportunities. By leveraging these technologies, disruptors can drive efficiency, improve decision-making, and create value in ways that were previously unimaginable.

Another important trend is the growing emphasis on sustainability and environmental stewardship. As the world grapples with the impacts of climate change and resource scarcity, there is an increasing demand for sustainable solutions that promote environmental and social responsibility. Disruptors who prioritize sustainability and integrate it into their business models will be at the forefront of driving positive change. By creating innovative solutions that address environmental challenges, disruptors can contribute to a more sustainable and equitable future.

The future of disruption will also be shaped by the evolving needs and preferences of consumers. As consumers become more informed and empowered, there is a growing expectation for personalized and seamless experiences. Disruptors who can anticipate and respond to these changing expectations will be well-positioned to drive innovation and create value. By staying attuned to consumer trends and leveraging data and technology, disruptors can create solutions that meet the evolving needs of their customers.

Ultimately, the future of disruption will be characterized by continuous innovation and transformation. Disruptive billionaires who embrace change and stay ahead of the curve will continue to drive revolutionary change and shape the global economy. By leveraging their visionary thinking, technological prowess, and ethical leadership, they can create a positive impact on society and leave a lasting legacy.

Book Description:

"The Disruption DNA: How Billionaires Code Industries for Revolution and Redraw the Globe" is an insightful exploration into the minds and strategies of the world's most influential disruptors. Through seventeen captivating chapters, this book delves into the core principles and practices that drive billionaires to challenge the status quo and create revolutionary change across industries.

Readers will discover the powerful combination of visionary thinking, technological prowess, and strategic risk-taking that sets disruptive billionaires apart. From understanding market dynamics and fostering innovation to building strong networks and navigating regulatory landscapes, this book provides a comprehensive guide to the art of disruption.

By examining real-world examples and drawing on the experiences of successful disruptors, "The Disruption DNA" offers valuable lessons and

CHAPTER 17: THE FUTURE OF DISRUPTION

practical insights for aspiring innovators and entrepreneurs. Whether you are looking to drive change in your industry or simply curious about the forces shaping our world, this book is an essential read for anyone interested in the future of innovation and disruption.

Dive into the world of disruptive billionaires and uncover the secrets to their success. Learn how they harness the power of technology, prioritize customer-centric innovation, and navigate the complexities of the global market. Discover the impact of disruption on society and the importance of ethical leadership and social responsibility. With "The Disruption DNA," you'll gain a deeper understanding of the forces driving revolutionary change and be inspired to create a lasting impact in your own endeavors.

www.ingramcontent.com/pod-product-compliance
Lightning Source LLC
LaVergne TN
LVHW020458080526
838202LV00057B/6031